30–
Rmc

Fighting Infectious Diseases

Robert Snedden

Heinemann LIBRARY

First published in Great Britain by Heinemann Library,
Halley Court, Jordan Hill, Oxford OX2 8EJ,
a division of Reed Educational and Professional Publishing Ltd.
Heinemann is a registered trademark of Reed Educational & Professional Publishing Limited.

OXFORD MELBOURNE AUCKLAND
JOHANNESBURG BLANTYRE GABORONE
IBADAN PORTSMOUTH NH (USA) CHICAGO

Produced by Paul Davies and Associates
Originated by Ambassador Litho Ltd
Printed in Hong Kong/China

04 03 02 01 00
10 9 8 7 6 5 4 3 2 1

ISBN 0 431 09274 5

British Library Cataloguing in Publication Data

Snedden, Robert
  Fighting infectious diseases. – (Microlife)
  1. Communicable diseases – Juvenile literature 2. Infection –
  Juvenile literature 3. Communicable diseases – Prevention –
  Juvenile literature
  I. Title
  616.9

  ISBN 0431092745

Acknowledgements
The Publishers would like to thank the following for permission to reproduce photographs:
Gamma: p45, M Schwarz p40; Image Select: p15, N Birch p24, World Health Organization pp12, 18, 19; Planet Earth Pictures: p31; Science Photo Library: T Brain p20, BSIP VEM pp7, 37, CNRI p23, J Durham p29, EM Unit, CVL Weybridge p14, S Fraser p39, A Gragera/Latin Stock p5, M Kage p4, J King-Holmes p42, Dr K Lounatmaa pp16, 26 M Meadows/Peter Arnold Inc p17, Moredun Animal Health Ltd p35, S Ogden p41, A Pasieka p9, B Yarvin p10; Tony Stone Images: M Jang p11; Telegraph Colour Library: J Burns p13, Planet Earth/Geof Du Feu p32, S Rowell p25.

Cover photograph reproduced with permission of Mehau Kulyk, Science Photo Library.

The Publishers would like to thank Dr Puran Ganeri for his comments in the preparation of this title.

Every effort has been made to contact copyright holders of any material reproduced in this book. Any omissions will be rectified in subsequent printings if notice is given to the Publisher.

For more information about Heinemann Library books, or to order, please phone ++44 (0)1865 888066, or send a fax to ++44 (0)1865 314091. You can visit our website at www.heinemann.co.uk.

Any words appearing in the text in bold, **like this**, are explained in the Glossary.

CONTENTS

INTRODUCTION   4

VIRUSES AND VECTORS   6

FIGHTING THE VIRUSES   8

IMMUNIZATION   10

AIDS-KILLER WITHOUT A CURE   12

RABIES-THE FEARSOME VIRUS   14

INFLUENZA-THE COMING EPIDEMIC?   16

SMALLPOX-A DISEASE DEFEATED   18

BACTERIAL DISEASES   20

BACTERIA AND BIOFILMS   22

ANTIBIOTICS   24

TUBERCULOSIS-RETURN OF A KILLER   26

INFECTIOUS FUNGI   28

PROTISTAN PARASITES   30

MALARIA-THE EFFICIENT KILLER   32

MALARIA-THE SEARCH FOR A SOLUTION   34

HELMINTH HORRORS   36

MICROBE MUTATIONS   38

EMERGING DISEASES   40

DNA VACCINES-THE SHAPE OF THINGS TO COME?   42

BIOLOGICAL WEAPONS   44

GLOSSARY   46

INDEX   48

INTRODUCTION

It is quite likely that you, or someone else you know, will become ill at some time in the next year. Most of us catch a cold at least once a year. You may remember having suffered in childhood from illnesses such as measles or chicken pox, or having seen a younger brother or sister come down with them. Someone in your family may have to take to bed with flu or, if they are very unlucky, be made ill by food poisoning.

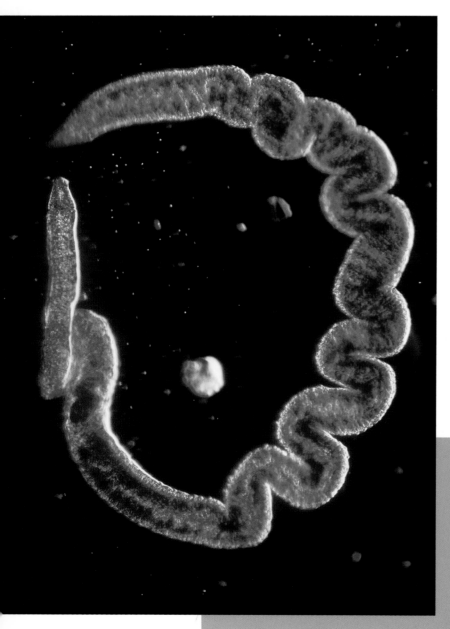

DISEASE AGENTS

Each of these **infectious** diseases is caused by a particular **micro-organism**, an invisibly small life form that can, as the name suggests, only be seen under a microscope. A micro-organism that causes infectious illness is called a **disease agent**. From the smallest to the largest, these range from **viruses** to **bacteria, fungi, protists** and **helminths** (**parasitic** worms).

An adult female fluke, a parasitic worm that causes the disease schistosomiasis, which kills around 200,000 people each year.

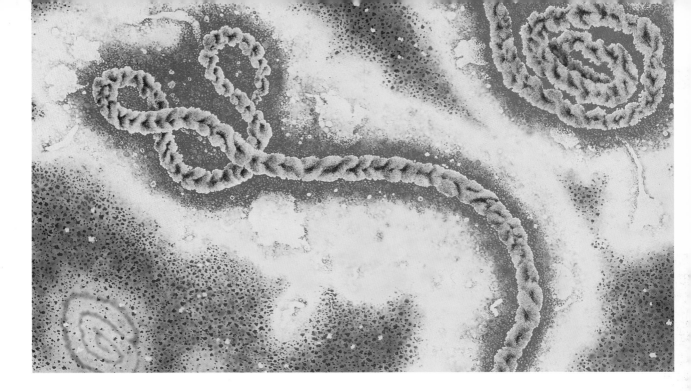

THE BATTLEGROUND

The number and variety of infectious diseases is formidable.
Malaria, hepatitis, cholera, AIDS, tuberculosis, sleeping sickness,
river blindness, Lassa fever and many more. Some, like the
common cold, are merely inconvenient; others, such as the
Ebola virus, are deadly. Some, such as AIDS, are relatively new,
while most are as old as humanity. Infectious disease is the
leading cause of death each year, causing about one-third of
all deaths throughout the world.

In this book we will look at disease agents, the effects they
have and how we can combat them. With so many disease-
causing agents all around us, it can sometimes appear
astounding that the human race has survived so long. After all,
it is only within the last 150 years that the connection
between micro-organisms and disease has become widely
accepted. We will also take a close look at our remarkable
immune system, the **cells** in our bodies that are dedicated to
fighting off micro-invaders, and at the problems we face in
dealing with bacteria that are becoming increasingly resistant
to our medicines.

The Ebola virus, the
cause of outbreaks of a
particularly severe, and
often fatal, fever in
parts of Africa in
recent years.

Viruses and Vectors

Viruses are simple but effective **disease agents**. Essentially, a virus is a set of instructions, for making a new virus, wrapped up in a protective coat. Viruses range in size from 20 to 200 millionths of a millimetre. The full stop at the end of the last sentence is probably around 0.5 millimetres across – so you can work out how many viruses could fit on it!

Viruses Revealed

Although the existence of viruses was suspected by the end of the 19th century, it was not until the electron microscope was perfected after the Second World War that people began to see what a virus looked like. Despite their small size, viruses come in a variety of shapes and cause diseases as diverse in their effects and seriousness as AIDS, rabies, polio, measles, influenza and the common cold.

Viruses themselves are not complete living organisms. They are true **parasites**, depending entirely on a living organism, called a host, for their needs. No parasite can afford to harm its host too much or to have its host develop an immunity, or resistance, to it. A virus that killed off 100 per cent of the people it attacked would soon die out itself when it ran out of new people to infect.

Reservoirs

A successful virus that has severe effects on one host will have another host, called a reservoir host, in which it produces milder effects. This ensures the virus's continued survival. For many human viruses, such as measles, herpes and influenza, the human population is its own reservoir as different people have different levels of resistance to these diseases.

Disease Vectors

The **vector** of a disease is the way in which it gets from one host to another. The transmission of diseases like influenza or

The Lassa fever virus. The virus is carried by rats and can be caught by humans who inhale rat urine, or from droplets coughed into the air by people already infected.

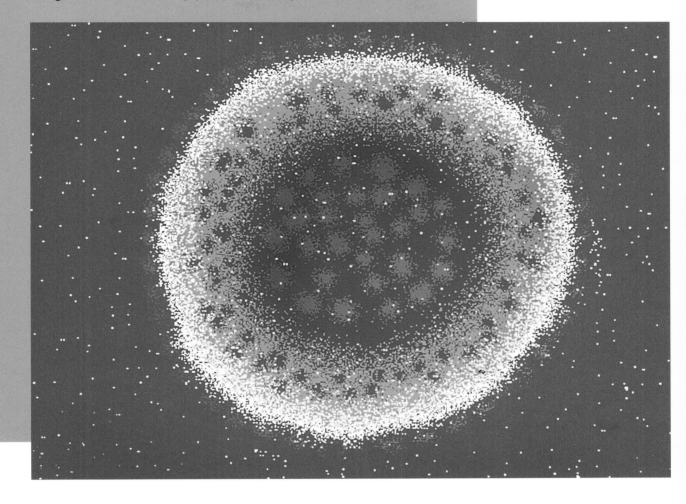

herpes is through the air or through close physical contact. Other diseases are carried by insects or other animals. Lassa fever, a disease that is often fatal in humans, is transmitted by rodents. Dengue fever, a serious disease of the tropics, is carried by a species of mosquito. Kuru, a 100 per cent fatal brain disease found only in New Guinea, was transmitted through a ceremony involving the eating of human brains! Since this habit is no longer followed, the disease – robbed of its vector – is disappearing.

FIGHTING THE VIRUSES

We are not entirely defenceless against the **viruses** that try to invade our **cells**. There are a couple of effective ways in which our bodies can counter virus attacks.

INTERFERONS

If a particular virus infects some of the cells in your body, the infected cells make substances called **interferons**. These are a type of **protein**. Interferons work with cells next to the site of the infection, helping them to become more resistant to the virus. Sometimes this works, sometimes not. If the resistance is not strong enough the virus continues to spread and affect more and more cells. The more cells it affects the sicker we feel.

THE IMMUNE SYSTEM

The next line of defence is the body's **immune system**. It begins to attack the viruses before they can penetrate the cells, and to kill cells that have become infected. Killing the infected cells is a bit like making a firebreak to stop a forest fire spreading. A virus needs a living cell in order to reproduce itself and the immune system kills the cells before the virus has managed to do this. Eventually, if the immune system does its job, the virus will be completely removed from the body and you will start to feel better.

ANTIBODIES

The body's most effective line of attack against viruses are its **antibodies**, **proteins** produced by the immune system. Antibodies stop the spread of a disease through the body. The antibody binds with the virus, making it harmless or destroying it altogether. The body makes large amounts of antibodies when a virus invader is detected. Antibodies are made in places such as the glands under the arm or the tonsils in the throat. This is why some diseases cause sore throats or lumps in the armpits. The glands there are busy pouring antibodies into the bloodstream to fight the virus. Antibodies have no effect against viruses once those viruses get inside cells.

IMMUNITY

Each disease brings about the production of a specific antibody to fight it. Some diseases, such as measles, will only ever make you ill once. This is because the measles antibodies stay in your bloodstream. If measles viruses ever attack again, they are dealt with so swiftly and effectively that you will never know they were there at all. You are said to have become immune to the disease, or developed an immunity.

This computer graphic shows the complex three-dimensional shape of the immunoglobin G1 antibody.

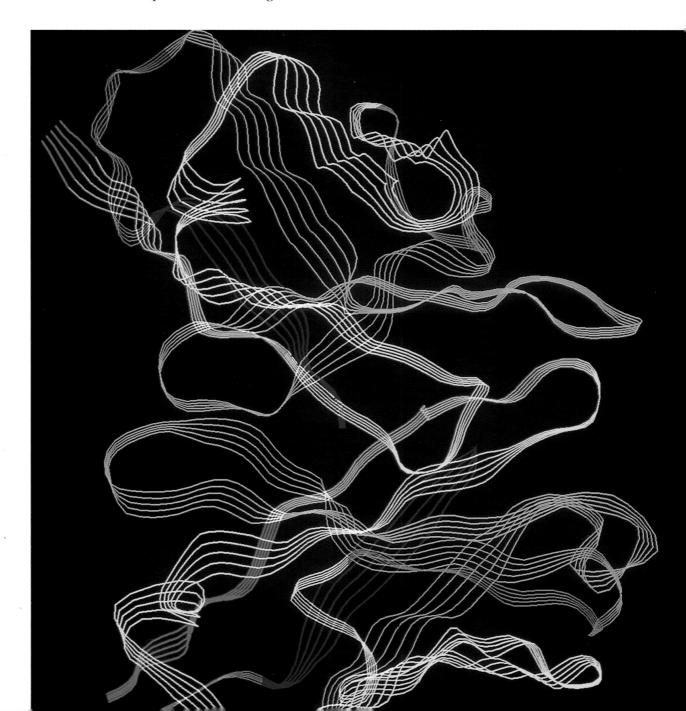

IMMUNIZATION

We can produce resistance to a disease without actually catching it. This is done by introducing a **vaccine** into the body.

VACCINES

A vaccine is a weakened or milder form of a **virus**. It will activate the body's production of **antibodies** but will not cause any disease **symptoms**. The presence of the antibodies gives immunity against the normal form of the virus. The process of giving immunity in this way is called **immunization**.

Another method is to use viruses that have been rendered inactive, for example by treating them with the chemical formaldehyde. These viruses are then introduced into the body as a 'killed' vaccine. Although the virus is inactive the **immune system** can still recognize it and is triggered to produce antibodies.

A hypodermic syringe is used to give accurately measured doses of vaccines.

PASSIVE IMMUNIZATION

Passive immunization is so-called because the person being immunized is not involved in making antibodies. Instead, an animal, such as a horse, is immunized. The antibodies that the horse produces are collected from its blood and purified. They are then injected into the human. The result is that the human acquires immediate immunity to the disease. Immunity acquired in this way is only temporary, however, as the body is not stimulated into making its own antibodies.

MOTHER AND BABY

Passive immunity occurs naturally when antibodies are transferred from the mother to the foetus through the placenta. A baby also gets antibodies through colostrum, which is found in breast milk.

Colostrum is an important natural source of antibodies that will help to protect the baby from infection. It is passed on through the mother's milk in the first few days of the baby's life.

VACCINATION

Vaccination is generally given by injection whatever the virus's natural route into the body might be. An exception to this is live polio vaccine, which is given orally, the virus's natural way of infecting the body. Another method that is sometimes used is an aerosol spray into the nose. Vaccines for measles, influenza and respiratory syncytial virus, an agent that causes the disease of childhood bronchiolitis, are sometimes administered in this way.

Only some vaccines give life-long protection. Others have to be repeated to remain effective.

AIDS-KILLER WITHOUT A CURE

The **virus** that causes acquired immune deficiency syndrome (AIDS) had, so far as we can guess, infected nearly 50 million people in the world by the end of the 20th century, and there were few signs that its spread was being stopped. As yet there is no cure – of those infected around 14 million have died so far.

WHAT IS AIDS?

AIDS is caused by the human immunodeficiency virus (HIV). There are two types of AIDS virus, HIV-1 and 2, and a number of closely related ape viruses, the SIVs (simian immunodeficiency viruses). HIV infects white blood **cells**, attacking their natural processes and turning them over to virus production. During this process, the cells die, depriving the body of one of its defences against infections.

A DEVELOPING CRISIS

In the western world the crisis of AIDS seems to have died down a little. If it cannot be cured, at least health awareness campaigns have kept the number of new infections down. In Africa, the probable home of the virus, and in much of Asia, the situation is very different. Millions of Asians and Africans are dying from a disease that is now ranked as the fourth biggest killer of the **microbe** world, taking more lives than malaria every year. Where did this killer disease come from?

AIDS is the cause of many millions of deaths in Africa and Asia.

SPECIES HOPPING

At the beginning of 1999 Dr Beatrice H Hahn and her colleagues at the University of Alabama announced their finding that the human immunodeficiency virus passed from a sub-species of chimpanzee to humans in a small region of western equatorial Africa about 50 years ago. The transmission most likely occurred when the animals were butchered and eaten. It was some years before the virus spread further.

Eventually it was carried throughout Africa, and one day an air traveller unknowingly became infected and carried the virus to North America, where, in the 1980s, it first came to the world's attention.

SHORTENED LIVES

In Botswana, Namibia, Swaziland and Zimbabwe, between a fifth and a quarter of people aged between 15 and 49 have HIV or AIDS. Between a fifth and a half of women monitored in Zimbabwe were found to be carrying the virus. Because of AIDS, children born in the early years of the 21st century can expect to live for perhaps 40 years. Without the virus their life expectancy might have been nearer 70.

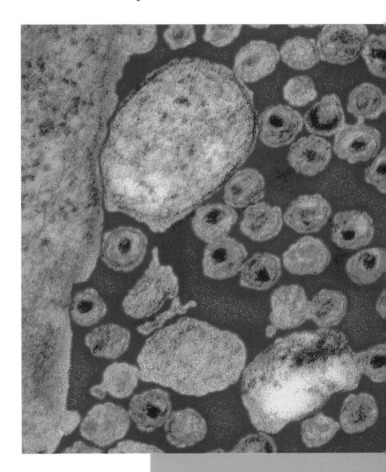

A MOVING TARGET

HIV **mutates** and **evolves** rapidly. This makes it very difficult to come up with an effective treatment. HIV is like a moving target because it changes all the time. A further complication arises because there are different varieties of HIV — each one of which may originally have come from a different ape or monkey species.

HIV can be passed on via infected body fluids. Sufferers can become infected through sexual intercourse, tranfusion of infected blood and the reuse of infected syringes.

RABIES-THE FEARSOME VIRUS

Rabies, also known as hydrophobia, is one of the most dreaded of all diseases. It is a **virus** disease of the central nervous system, the brain and spinal cord, that afflicts warm-blooded animals, especially the dog family. It is transmitted to humans through contamination with the infected saliva of rabid animals. It is nearly always fatal.

PATHWAY TO THE BRAIN

The connection between rabies and the bite of a rabid animal has been known for centuries. The disease is caused by a virus that is concentrated in the saliva of the affected animal. It is transmitted by a bite, or a lick if the affected animal licks a cut or graze. Once inside the body the virus travels along the nerves towards the central nervous system. Unlike many other **disease agents** it does not use the bloodstream as a means of transport.

THE SYMPTOMS

Once infection has taken place the time it takes for the **symptoms** to appear varies according to how badly bitten the victim was and where the bites are. Exceptionally, it might take a year. On average, symptoms appear in about 30 days following face bites, 40 days after arm bites and about 60 days after leg bites.

The deadly rabies virus, which is transmitted to humans by the bite of an infected animal.

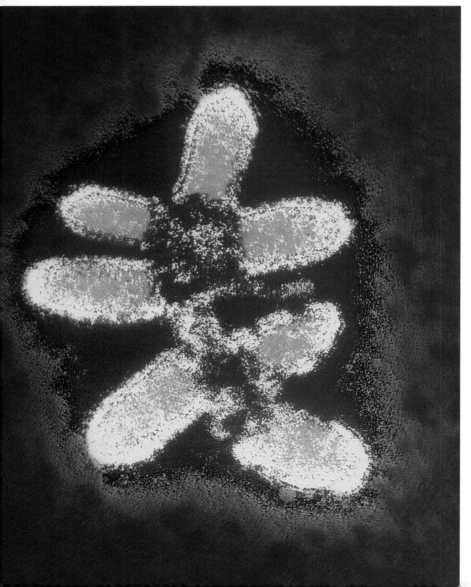

Early symptoms include pain in the bite area, headache, slight fever, nausea, restlessness, anxiety, depression and rapid speech. As the disease takes hold restlessness, apprehension and discomfort increase. Muscle spasms prevent the swallowing of food or water, although the victim will experience an intense thirst and become dehydrated. Death usually comes around the third day of this phase.

HYDROPHOBIA

Muscle spasms may occur at the mere sight or sound of water, the source of rabies other name, hydrophobia, which means fear of water.

THE TREATMENT

Once symptoms develop, rabies is almost always fatal. There is no treatment that is guaranteed to succeed. The wounds must be washed thoroughly and then disinfected with carbolic or nitric acid if possible. Antirabies **vaccine** has greatly reduced the death rate from rabies but it is not universally effective. It is costly and there may be unfortunate side effects, including paralysis. **Vaccination** must start at once and daily injections are given for two to three weeks. An antirabies serum was developed in the 1950s and a combined serum-vaccine treatment seems to have the highest success rate. Some people have a natural immunity to the virus and will not develop the disease, even if a bite from a rabid animal is left untreated.

Rabies vaccination being carried out at the Pasteur Institute around 1910. The treatment at that time involved painful injections into the abdomen.

QUARANTINE

Prevention would appear to be better than cure as far as rabies is concerned. For example, strict **quarantine** laws have prevented the disease crossing into Britain from Europe and have also kept it out of Australia.

INFLUENZA-THE COMING EPIDEMIC?

In the years following the First World War, the planet was struck by a **virus epidemic** that was more devastating, in terms of the number of deaths, than the plague of medieval times. It began on 4 March 1918, when the first case was reported in Kansas, USA. Within four months millions of people around the world had fallen ill. Few died of the disease and most attention was focused on the approaching end of the war.

KILLER SWITCH

In September 1918, the relatively mild virus that had spread around the world changed into something that was much more deadly. In an almost simultaneous triple strike, the new strain hit France, Sierra Leone and Boston, USA. Those infected died in huge numbers, drowning as fluid filled their lungs. Appalled doctors thought that this strange new disease might be an airborne version of the Black Death. The virus spread rapidly. In six months, from September 1918 to March 1919, it killed over 33,000 people in New York City alone. By the time the epidemic had run its course an estimated 30 million people had died world-wide, many more than had been killed in the four years of fighting in the war. For some reason, still unknown, the virus was particularly dangerous among young adults.

Influenza viruses. Tiny spikes on the outside of the viruses help them to stick to the **cells** they attack.

The cause of this epidemic was the influenza virus, although at the time no one knew that a virus caused flu. The 1918 strain of influenza persisted for a few years and then simply disappeared, or changed into a form that was not so **virulent**. Questions are still being asked as to what made this virus so deadly. Could it happen again?

The droplets expelled in a sneeze may carry viruses that can spread infectious diseases such as influenza.

CATCHING THE FLU

Influenza is transmitted from human-to-human through the air. The virus infects the mucous membranes lining the upper respiratory tract. Fever, chills, fatigue and headache may last up to a week, and then recovery is usually rapid. Influenza epidemics occur when a new and highly virulent virus **strain** arises. Viruses change all the time. As they make billions of copies of themselves mistakes are made. Some result in a weakened or non-functioning virus, others may make it stronger.

VIRUS GENE EXCHANGE

Viruses can also trade **genes** with each other producing new strains that are so different from the ones around before that humans have no immunity to them. We actually increase the danger of new viruses emerging because of agricultural, industrial and social practices. New strains of flu have spread world-wide from China, for example. The virus arose there because farmers raised pigs and ducks together. A bird flu virus from the ducks infected the pigs. Inside the pig **cells** the bird virus exchanged genes with mammalian viruses. The new strains of influenza eventually infected the farmers.

Smallpox-a Disease Defeated

Smallpox has afflicted humans since prehistoric times. It is highly **contagious** and repeated **pandemics** have circled the world. It is often fatal and is characterized by high fever and a blistering rash, which usually leaves permanent scarring if the victim survives. In the 18th century it was a particular scourge in Europe and North America.

Smallpox was a terrible disease, producing a painful blistering rash on the skin of victims.

Edward Jenner

It was the search for an effective treatment for smallpox that led Edward Jenner to discover **vaccination** in 1796. Jenner discovered that he could safely give immunity from smallpox by vaccinating patients with matter from cowpox, a **virus** disease of cattle that is related to smallpox but completely harmless to humans. Cowpox, or *vaccinia* in Latin, gave its name to vaccination. Over the next century and a half variations on Jenner's procedure, using different vaccines, protected countless humans against **bacterial** diseases such as typhoid, cholera and tetanus, and viral illnesses such as yellow fever and polio. Thanks to Jenner, smallpox became rarer and less **virulent**.

Smallpox Symptoms

The incubation period of smallpox, the time from the introduction of the virus into the body to when **symptoms** start to show, is generally eleven to twelve days. The victim is highly contagious, especially when the rash develops. The virus is found on the skin, in the throat, and in the urine and faeces. It may also persist on clothing and bedding. Infection can be spread through the air and by direct contact. There is no natural immunity to the disease – any non-vaccinated person exposed to smallpox will be infected by it. Babies are particularly vulnerable to the disease.

The symptoms of smallpox are similar to those of influenza to begin with: high temperature, headache, muscle pains, chills and, often, vomiting. When the rash appears on about the fourth day, however, smallpox can be definitely diagnosed. The skin becomes sprinkled with spots and these become filled with fluid that is first clear, then becomes pus. In severe cases the spots leave permanent, disfiguring pockmarks.

THE END OF THE DISEASE

In 1967 the World Health Organization (WHO) of the United Nations began a world-wide programme aimed at completely eradicating smallpox. Thirteen years later, after an intensive campaign of vaccination and **quarantine**, WHO announced that naturally occurring smallpox had been totally eliminated from the world. The only deaths now caused by smallpox are isolated instances resulting from laboratory accidents. The last known case occurred in 1978.

A programme of **immunization** carried out by the World Health Organization has seen the end of smallpox.

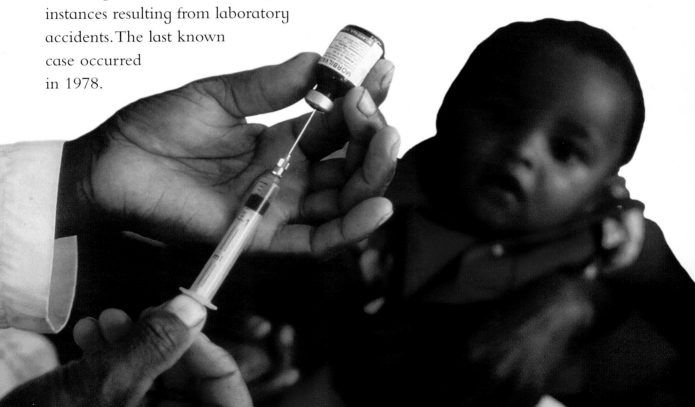

BACTERIAL DISEASES

We share our surroundings, and indeed our bodies, with a bewildering number and variety of **bacteria**. There are more bacterial **cells** in and on your body than there are cells making you up! Fortunately, most of them are harmless and some are even helpful.

SIZES AND SHAPES

Bacteria can be shaped like rods (called bacilli), spheres (called cocci) or spirals (called spirilla), and vary in size from 1 to 20 thousandths of a millimetre in length, which makes them quite a bit bigger than **viruses**. Bacteria can be found as single cells, clusters of cells, or may form chains that can be either branched or straight. These differences in appearance are useful in classifying the different members of the bacterial kingdom.

Certain bacteria are able to form **spores**, which are extremely resistant to chemicals, heat, cold or drying out. Bacteria grow and multiply in simple **nutrient** solutions, soils and natural waters, as well as in living organisms. Disease-causing bacteria grow in human organs and cause illness either by invading tissues or by producing **toxins**, or poisons, that are harmful to certain organs or body functions. The **symptoms** of bacterial illness can range from mild uneasiness or brief illness to rapid death.

NUMBER ONE KILLER

Tuberculosis, cholera and tetanus are among the serious diseases caused by bacteria. Tuberculosis, indeed, is the number one cause of death by **infectious microbe**.

FOOD POISONING

Food poisoning can be caused either by eating food containing bacterial toxins made in the food by bacteria, or by the growth in the body of bacteria that contaminated the food. *Staphylococcus aureus* can grow in creamed foods that are not properly refrigerated. Vomiting and diarrhoea occur a few hours after it is ingested. *Clostridium perfringens* grows readily in warm meat. Bacteria that get into the body produce spores in the intestines. This releases a toxin that causes diarrhoea within a day of the contaminated food being consumed.

Salmonella species may contaminate meat, poultry and dairy products. The source of contamination is either the animal itself or the food handlers. If the food is not properly cooked before eating, the bacteria infect the intestinal tract and cause fever, vomiting and diarrhoea.

CHOLERA

The most serious waterborne bacterial disease is cholera, caused by *Vibrio cholerae*. Cholera poisons cause severe diarrhoea that can result in the loss of 20 litres of fluid per day and death by dehydration. Cholera occurs where sewage is not properly treated. Infection normally occurs through drinking contaminated water.

Bacteria are everywhere. This colony is growing on the tip of a syringe needle used to give injections.

BACTERIA AND BIOFILMS

Some **bacteria** can actually work together to form strong communities called **biofilms**. A biofilm consists of billions upon billions of **micro-organisms** living on the surface of something that can provide the bacteria with water and **nutrients**. It is something like a microscopic city in which the bacteria are joined together to form multicellular columns.

BRUSH OFF THE BIOFILM

If you reach into your mouth you may be able to touch a biofilm. The plaque that forms on your teeth if you don't brush regularly is a biofilm. Biofilms also form on badly cleaned contact lenses and can lead to eye infections.

SLIMES

When bacteria form biofilms the **cell** walls of the individual bacteria become tougher and more difficult to penetrate. Biofilms are sometimes called slimes because the bacteria produce a coat of slimy material that helps protect them. A biofilm can be 1500 times more resistant to **antibiotics** than a simple colony of bacteria. Some biofilms are even resistant to powerful chlorine-based disinfectants.

PSEUDOMONAS AERUGINOSA

Pseudomonas aeruginosa is a common bacterium that forms biofilms. It can be found on fruit, vegetables and in the soil. Individually, the cells can be controlled by antibiotics but when they form biofilms they become that much harder to fight and an infection can become untreatable and deadly. White blood cells, which could normally consume individual bacteria, can do nothing to attack a biofilm. The *Pseudomonas aeruginosa* bacterium commonly affects people whose **immune systems** have been damaged; for example burn victims are often affected. *Pseudomonas aeruginosa* biofilms may also become attached to devices implanted in the body such as heart valves, causing them to fail.

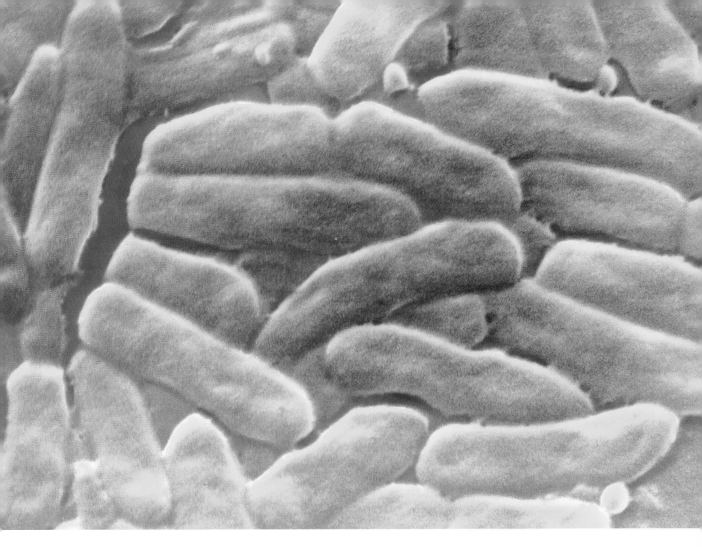

SIGNAL BLOCKING

Currently scientists are looking for ways to stop the formation of biofilms by disrupting the chemical 'conversations' that go on between the bacteria when they are forming their columns. The hope is that if the signalling process can be understood, then ways to block the signals can be developed. It is possible that by preventing the formation of biofilms a way could be found to prevent dental plaque and other health problems.

BIOFILM BUDDIES

Biofilms aren't all bad. Some are formed from harmless bacteria that line the insides of our intestines and give some protection from harmful disease-causing organisms.

Pseuodomonas aeruginosa, a bacterium that is found in hospitals where it can infect people already weakened by illness or injury.

ANTIBIOTICS

Antibiotics are substances that kill or restrict the growth of **bacteria** and **fungi**. They can be used to help the body fight infection from these **micro-organisms**. Antibiotics have no effect on **viruses**.

MICROSCOPIC ARMS RACE

'Antibiosis', which means against life, was coined in the 19th century to describe a type of natural competition among different species of **microbe**. Antibiotics are produced naturally by various forms of bacteria and fungi as a means of gaining an advantage in the competition for space and resources. When we use antibiotics we are simply making use of one micro-organism's natural means of attacking another.

PENICILLIN

Today, many different antibiotics are used to treat infections and millions of lives have been saved since antibiotics were first used in 1941. Penicillin, the first antibiotic to be discovered (by Alexander Fleming in 1928), is perhaps still the best known. It is named after *Penicillium notatum*, the mould that produces it. We now have a number of other antibiotics, all of which are effective against different bacterial and fungal diseases.

THE GROWING RESISTANCE

People are becoming concerned because many disease-causing bacteria are becoming resistant to the effects of antibiotics.

Penicillium moulds are the most widespread known and will colonize exposed foods. This mould is growing on a tomato

Antibiotic-resistant bacteria are a growing problem around the world. Although they are not yet widespread in the general population, they are becoming more common in hospitals, particularly in patients who have been treated with many drugs over a long period. Many patients do not finish their courses of antibiotics because they feel better before getting to the end of the treatment. This leaves some bacteria alive, and these bacteria are the ones most likely to pass resistance to the antibiotic on to the next generation of bacteria.

THE NEXT GENERATION

Scientists are working to develop a new generation of antibiotics for treating the growing number of resistant bacteria. However, it seems likely that the bacteria will continue to **evolve** and adapt to whatever we throw at them. Many doctors now think that antibiotic use should be restricted. They blame over-prescription of antibiotics in the past, saying that this has given bacteria the opportunity to develop resistance. Resistance to an antibiotic can spread swiftly through a population of bacteria because they have the ability to exchange **genetic** material and pass resistance on to each other.

Scientists are working constantly to develop new treatments for bacteria as they become resistant to present-day antibiotics.

ANTIBIOTICS IN FARMING

The widespread use of antibiotics in farm animals has also helped the spread of drug-resistant bacteria. Farmers began feeding animals antibiotics to promote growth and prevent infection. Inevitably the bacteria in the animals became more drug-resistant and this has led to hazards such as the appearance of drug-resistant salmonella, one of the causes of food poisoning. Salmonella is spread through eating incompletely cooked meat, poultry or eggs.

TUBERCULOSIS-RETURN OF A KILLER

Tuberculosis, or TB, is caused by a **bacterium** called *Mycobacterium tuberculosis.* The **symptoms** are coughs, weight loss, night sweats, fever, chest pains and coughing up blood. Tuberculosis spreads through airborne droplets sprayed out whenever an infected person coughs. These can remain in the air for around two hours, to be breathed in by someone else who will be infected in turn.

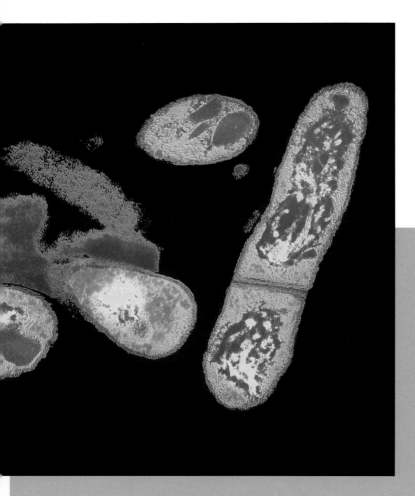

Mycobacterium tuberculosis, the cause of tuberculosis in humans. New drug-resistant strains of the bacterium are bringing the return of a disease that was once thought to have been beaten.

THE FORGOTTEN DISEASE

Tuberculosis is a disease that has largely been forgotten in the major industrialized countries of the world. It is often thought of as something that happened in the past. In the early 1800s, it was a major cause of death.

EMOTIONAL ILLNESS

It was once believed that tuberculosis was caused by an excess of emotions!

THE ANTIBIOTIC ANSWER

In 1865, Jean Antoine Villemin demonstrated scientifically that tuberculosis was an **infectious** illness and, in 1882, Robert Koch identified *Mycobacterium tuberculosis* as the **disease agent**. Once it was known that tuberculosis was **contagious**, measures were taken to prevent its spread. These included isolating infected people in sanatoriums and attempting to improve living conditions in towns and cities. In 1908 the BCG **vaccination** was developed, giving children immunity from the disease. By the middle years of the 20th century effective **antibiotics** that treated and cured most cases had been developed. Across Europe and the United States tuberculosis was being defeated, or so it seemed.

TB ON THE RISE

in the mid-1980s, the number of reported tuberculosis infections began to increase steadily around the world. One important cause has been the emergence of new forms, or **strains**, of the original bacterium that are resistant to most of the drugs once used to treat it. This is sometimes called MDR-TB, or multiple drug resistant tuberculosis. Around the world tuberculosis kills between 2 and 3 million people every year, more than any other infectious disease. In March 1998, the World Health Organization issued a warning that TB could infect 1 billion more people in the next 20 years and that 70 million of them are likely to die.

FIGHTING BACK

Some progress has been made against tuberculosis and work is being done to develop a drug that is effective against the new resistant TB strains. TB, however, attracts fewer resources than some diseases. The reason, unfortunately, is that it tends to be a disease of the poor – hungry people have less resistance to the disease. As people in the drug industry have admitted, the people in the most affected areas are those least able to pay for treatment. The result is that drugs to fight TB are low on the list of priorities.

INFECTIOUS FUNGI

Fungi will grow on any wet material, be it indoors or outdoors, and on moist parts of the human body. Fungi can cause disease in three ways. They can produce an allergic reaction in sensitive individuals; they produce poisons called mycotoxins; and they can invade and grow in or on the body.

MYCOSIS

The growth of a fungus on or in the body is called **mycosis**. Fungal infections often take hold after the use of **antibiotics**. These drugs get rid of the body's harmless bacteria as well as the disease-causing varieties and this leaves a 'space' for fungal or other invaders to fill. The **immune system** of normally healthy people is sufficiently powerful to prevent invasion by nearly all fungi.

Many fungal infections affect only the outer layers of skin, and although they are annoying and sometimes difficult to cure, they are not life-threatening. Athlete's foot is a common fungal infection, but perhaps the best-known of the infectious fungi are the candida yeasts. These can grow and become a problem in the digestive or urinary tracts of the body.

INTERNAL INFECTIONS

Fungi that affect the deeper layers of skin and internal organs can cause serious, sometimes fatal, illness. Cryptococcus is a type of fungus that can cause a form of meningitis, an inflammation of the meninges (the membrane that encloses the brain). For some reason it affects men twice as often as women. It can also affect the lungs, causing coughs and fever, or spread to the nervous system. There is no reliable treatment for this infection and it is usually fatal. *Cryptococcus neoformans*, the **disease agent**, has been found in pigeon droppings.

Sporotrichosis is an infection found in those who come into regular contact with plants and soil, such as farmers. The disease affects the skin and lymphatic system. It is rarely fatal.

Histoplasmosis

Histoplasmosis is a severe fungal infection that can cause a wide variety of **symptoms**. In acute cases ulcers form inside the throat and the liver and **spleen** become enlarged. In other forms of the infection the lungs can become damaged, developing injuries similar to those caused by tuberculosis. Sometimes no disease symptoms are apparent at all and the infection is usually discovered accidentally when the chest is X-rayed.

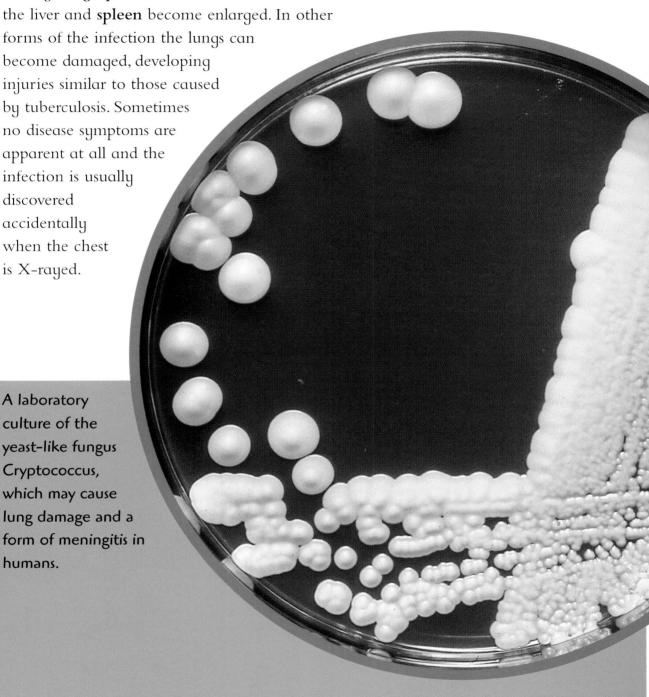

A laboratory culture of the yeast–like fungus Cryptococcus, which may cause lung damage and a form of meningitis in humans.

PROTISTAN PARASITES

The **protists** are single-celled life forms that occur in a great variety of shapes and sizes, ranging from 2 to 100 thousandths of a millimetre. One of the best known, and deadliest, protists are the group of four Plasmodium species that cause malaria. Plasmodium's complex life cycle, which we will examine later, involves multi-stage development in humans, coupled with further development in the gut of a female mosquito.

LEISHMANIASIS

Other problem protists include the Leishmania species. Dogs and rodents act as a reservoir for the **parasites**. They are transmitted to humans by the bite of female sandflies, which pick up the infection when they bite animals. Leishmaniasis takes many forms, from self-healing ulcers to terrible destruction of facial features when the parasites invade the membranes of the nose and mouth. One feature of the Leishmania parasites that makes them difficult to deal with is that they actually invade the white blood **cells** that are normally responsible for dealing with **microbe** invaders. More than 12 million people are afflicted with this disease.

THE BLACK SICKNESS

The most dangerous form of leishmaniasis is commonly referred to as *kala-azar*, a Hindi term meaning 'black sickness'. The name describes the increased discolouring of the skin that is typical of the disease. If left untreated, *kala-azar* is invariably fatal.

A tsetse fly on a person's arm. The insect is the carrier of the parasitic trypanosome that causes sleeping sickness in humans.

SLEEPING SICKNESS

African trypanosomiasis, or 'sleeping sickness', is caused by a
type of parasite called a trypanosome. These trypanosomes are
transmitted to humans by the bite of tsetse flies. Initial
symptoms include fever, headache, dizziness and weakness.
Later, when the parasites invade the central nervous system,
hallucinations, delusions and seizures affect the victim. If
untreated, the patient may lapse into a coma and eventually
die. This disease affects some 25,000 people every year.

MASTER OF DISGUISE

An intriguing feature of the sleeping sickness trypanosome is its
ability to repeatedly change the **protein** that covers its surface.
By doing this it wrong-foots the ability of the victim's **immune
system** to identify it and produce **antibodies** against it. The
complex **genetic** mechanism that allows the parasite to do this
is not yet understood.

Malaria—The Efficient Killer

Every twelve seconds someone in the world dies from malaria — that is 2.7 million people every year, and most of them are children under five. Up to 500 million people are infected at any one time. The cause of this terrible disease is a **parasitic protist** called Plasmodium.

Mosquitoes and Malaria

The **vector** for malaria is the Anopheles mosquito. The female mosquito sucks blood by inserting her proboscis, the insect's slender feeding tube, through her victim's skin. As she does so her saliva is injected into the human's bloodstream. If the mosquito is infected with Plasmodium the saliva will contain thousands of tiny thread–like parasites called sporozoites.

A Complex Life Cycle

The sporozoites make their way to the liver, where they form **spores** in the liver **cells** and begin to multiply. Two weeks later, the liver cells burst, releasing huge numbers of spores, now called merozoites, into the bloodstream. It is when this happens that the sufferer begins to feel very ill. Each merozoite attacks and invades a red blood cell, feeding and growing inside it until

The female Anopheles mosquito is the carrier of the plasmodium parasite that is the cause of malaria. The parasite is transmitted to the human victim when the mosquito bites.

it is half the size of the cell. Then, it suddenly splits into 24 new merozoites that burst the blood cell apart and emerge to attack new blood cells. Up to 70 per cent of the victim's red blood cells could be colonized by the parasite.

HITCHING A RIDE

Some of the merozoites separate into male and female stages called gametocytes and migrate to blood vessels in the skin where they wait for a female mosquito to return. When the mosquito feeds, she sucks up a mouthful of gametocytes. The gametocytes breed in the mosquito's stomach forming tiny cysts on the outer surface. Two or three weeks later thousands of little sporozoites burst out and make their way into the mosquito's salivary gland ready to infect another human with the mosquito's next bite.

PLASMODIUM EVASIONS

Plasmodium has adapted itself very efficiently for life in its human and mosquito hosts. It manages to evade the body's defences with ease. Once injected by the mosquito's saliva, the parasites take only half an hour to get inside the liver cells. This isn't enough time for the **antibodies** in the bloodstream to attack and kill them all. The next line of defence is the killer T cells, part of the **immune system**, which hunt down and kill cells that have been invaded. The trouble is that it takes ten to twelve days for this response to kick in. Before this happens the parasite leaves the liver cells and attacks the red blood cells, and red blood cells do not trigger the T cell response.

Plasmodium is always one step ahead. As the parasites develop inside your red blood cells, they produce tiny knobs on the surface of the cells that cause the infected red blood cells to stick to the lining of the smallest blood vessels. The result is that the infected red blood cells are kept out of the **spleen**, which would recognize them as damaged cells and destroy them.

Malaria—The Search for a Solution

Malaria infections are not permanent. The most serious of the malarial strains will kill up to half the people it infects if left untreated. Those who survive will eventually rid themselves of the disease over a period of three to five years. Unfortunately, if they live in a malaria-infected area, they are likely to become reinfected. Around one-third of the world's population live in malarial areas. This means millions of people live in a perpetually weakened condition, with their resistance to other infections seriously reduced.

False Hopes

For a few decades after the Second World War malaria seemed to be on the retreat. Quinine, derived from the bark of the cinchona tree, and chloroquine, a similar **synthetic compound** were effective treatments. DDT insecticide sprays were used to kill the mosquito that carried the Plasmodium **parasite**. Then nature caught up — the parasite and mosquito became immune to the chemicals being thrown at them. Malaria came back stronger than before. There were three times as many cases of malaria in the 1990s as there had been in the 1960s.

Searching for a Vaccine

Immunologists trying to find a **vaccine** to defeat malaria find themselves facing many problems. Unlike a **virus** or a **bacterium**, which more or less stay the same, the malaria parasite goes through four stages of development in a human (see pages 32–33). A vaccine that is effective against the sporozoites might have no effect on the liver or blood stages, for example. In addition, an anti-malaria vaccine would have to be extraordinarily efficient. It takes just one or two sporozoites to survive to produce tens of thousands of merozoites in the liver.

Weakened Parasites

A possible solution would be to create a vaccine of weakened parasites, but this faces more problems. The sporozoites will only grow inside mosquitoes; the liver stages only inside human liver **cells**; and the merozoites in red blood cells. It is difficult for researchers to get enough of the parasites to work on. One option that seems to work is to take a mosquito infected with sporozoites and dose it with **radiation**. The parasites inside the mosquito are weakened by this treatment. Once in the human bloodstream they will still travel to the liver but they will not produce merozoites and colonize the red blood cells. They remain in the liver where they trigger a response from the **immune system**. The next time a healthy malaria parasite gets into the blood, the immune system is geared up and ready to deal with it.

DNA VACCINE

Recently, tests have been carried out using a 'DNA vaccine'. This involves injecting a person with the **gene** that makes the sporozoite's protective **protein** coat. There is more about DNA vaccines on page 44. The effect is to trigger the production of **antibodies** that will attack living sporozoites. However, a reliable vaccine still seems a distant prospect.

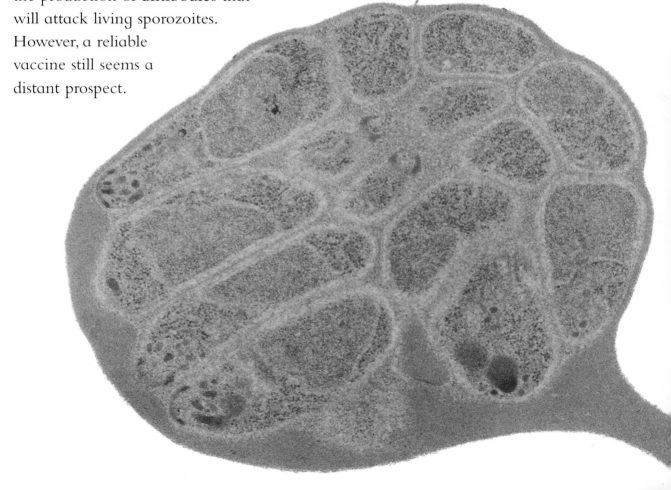

A red blood cell infected by merozoites. These will burst from the cell, destroying it as they do so, and go on to infect more cells.

HELMINTH HORRORS

The largest and most complex of the **infectious disease agents** are the multicellular **helminths**. These have complex life cycles that may involve microscopic eggs and larvae and larger adult stages.

THE MOST COMMON PARASITE?

Ascaris worms are probably the most common **parasite** in the world. They are found in temperate as well as tropical regions. Infection can cause abdominal pain and lack of weight gain in children and sometimes results in obstruction in the intestines.

TAPEWORMS

The tapeworm causes serious disease. Usually, people are infected by eating undercooked pork that contains the larval form of the parasite. The larvae develop into adult worms in the victim's intestine. Eggs leave the body in the faeces and may be eaten by pigs to continue the parasite's life cycle. When eggs are inadvertently eaten by people, the larvae may infect the central nervous system, causing serious disorders, including seizures. This disease is a serious problem in rural parts of Latin America.

THE BIGGEST DISEASE AGENT

Intestinal tapeworms are the largest of the disease agents, growing to lengths of 3 to 10 metres in human intestines.

BLOOD FLUKES

Schistosomiasis, a major disease that affects more than 200 million people in Africa, Asia, and South America, is caused by blood flukes, a type of flatworm. Around 200,000 people die every year with many more (about 10 per cent of those infected) suffering damage to vital organs such as the liver and kidneys.

SNAIL VECTOR

Schistosomiasis is interesting because it is not transmitted through the bite of an insect. The larvae develop within freshwater snails. After leaving the snail the larvae swim along until they contact a human host bathing or working in the water. They penetrate the skin, then migrate through the blood vessels. Adult flukes 6 to 20 millimetres in length take up residence in the veins of the intestine, liver or bladder, depending on the parasite species. The adult male and female worms pair, mate and produce large numbers of eggs. Some of the eggs they release become lodged in the organs, causing scar tissue to form. This scar tissue can block blood vessels, causing them to **rupture**. This can prove fatal. Eggs that are shed in faeces or urine enter the water and develop into larvae in fresh-water snails. They then exit into the water, where they swim until they find a human to start the cycle again.

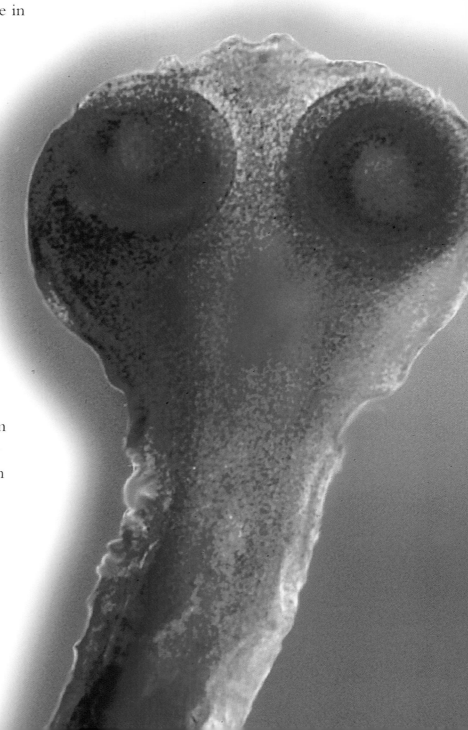

A tapeworm. showing the suckers with which it attaches itself to the lining of the intestines.

MICROBE MUTATIONS

One of the things that can make **infectious** diseases so hard to deal with is the speed with which they can change. Like the rest of the living world, **bacteria** and **viruses** are constantly **evolving**. The difference is that a generation for a bacterium might be just 20 minutes. This is like you having great grandchildren within an hour of being born. This rapid turnover allows resistant **strains** to emerge quickly.

MUTATIONS

A **mutation** is a change in the **genetic** material, or genes, of an organism. It can happen when a **cell's DNA** is copied before the cell divides. Sometimes mistakes are made when the DNA is replicated. Most mutations are either of no consequence, and so are never noticed, or they are disastrous and the mutant organism does not survive. Every now and then, however, a mutation occurs that gives the organism an advantage, something that makes it better able to survive in its environment. When this happens the organism can pass on the advantage to the next generation.

SHARING GOOD FORTUNE

Bacteria can sometimes share their good mutations with other bacteria they happen to meet. Resistance to an **antibiotic**, for example, can be passed from bacterium to bacterium by way of circular pieces of DNA called **plasmids**.

STAYING THE COURSE

Unwittingly we often help the strongest strains to survive. If you have a bacterial infection you will be infected by both strong and weak strains of the bacteria. Taking a course of an antibiotic will wipe out the weaker bacteria first and the more resistant strains will fill the gaps. If you do not finish the course of treatment – and many people don't – what's left are the toughest bacteria. When they go on to infect someone else they will be that much harder to shift.

AN EPIDEMIC OF RESISTANCE

By 1993 it was reckoned that nearly every common disease-causing bacterial species had developed some degree of drug resistance. More than two dozen of these emergent strains were potentially life-threatening and resistant to most commonly available antibiotic treatments. One scientist called it, 'an **epidemic** of **microbial** resistance'.

MUTANT TRAVELLER

A single mutant bacterium can give rise to a strain that spreads over the world within just a few years. In the 1970s a streptococcus infection struck children in hospitals in South Africa. When the bacterial strain was analysed it was found to match one that had been discovered in a remote village in New Guinea ten years earlier. How it reached South Africa remains a mystery, but eventually it got all around the world.

This doctor is examining the lymph glands in a patient's neck. Lymph nodes form part of the body's **immune system** and swelling of the glands indicates that they are fighting infection. Although medical science is advancing all the time, our immune systems are constantly having to deal with new mutations of known diseases.

Emerging Diseases

Emerging diseases are those that are new to us, those that are reappearing after a period of decline and those that are developing resistance to drugs. The emerging **infectious** diseases include all major types of **disease agents**. In 1992 the United States Institute of Medicine listed 54 emerging diseases. These included 26 emergent **viruses**, 17 emergent **bacteria**, and 11 emergent **protists**, **helminths** and **fungi**.

Defining Diseases

New diseases become known to us through the **symptoms** they produce. When someone becomes ill doctors decide what the disease is from the symptoms they see. If the symptoms match no known disease they might indicate that a new disease is at work and that a new disease agent has to be identified.

Unknown Killers

According to one recent estimate, in 14 per cent of deaths caused by infection of people aged from 1 to 49 in the United States, no known **microbe** could be identified as the cause.

Making an Identification

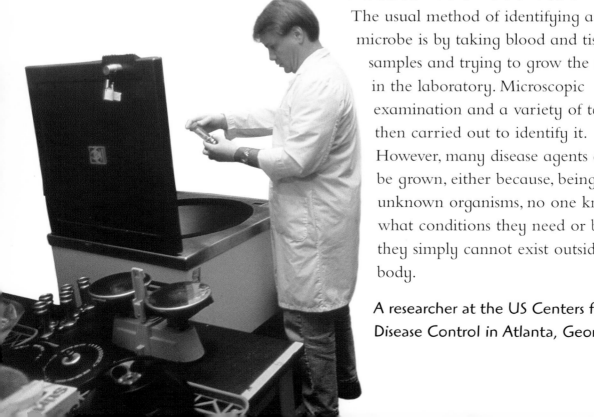

The usual method of identifying a microbe is by taking blood and tissue samples and trying to grow the microbe in the laboratory. Microscopic examination and a variety of tests are then carried out to identify it. However, many disease agents cannot be grown, either because, being unknown organisms, no one knows what conditions they need or because they simply cannot exist outside the body.

A researcher at the US Centers for Disease Control in Atlanta, Georgia.

ON THE FRONT LINE

The Unexplained Illness Working Group, set up by the US Centers for Disease Control and Prevention (CDC) in 1994 is at the forefront of the hunt for new disease agents. Hundreds of cases of unexplained illness can be under investigation at any time. Powerful new technologies are used to identify microbes by examining their **genetic** material. There is always the possibility that one of these unknown agents could emerge as the next HIV, or a deadly **strain** of influenza. New disease agents identified in the last quarter of the 20th century have included Ebola, Hanta and HIV. Other diseases once thought to have been defeated, such as tuberculosis, are reappearing in new **antibiotic**-resistant forms.

A researcher in a biologically secure laboratory at the Harvard Medical School. Here, dangerous viruses such as HIV are studied.

LEGIONNAIRE'S DISEASE

In 1976 people attending an American Legion convention in Philadelphia started falling ill. Doctors suspected at first that the cause was swine flu. CDC researchers worked for eight months before they realized that the cause was actually a previously unknown bacterium. The new disease was called Legionnaire's disease, after its first identified victims.

With the speed of travel around the world today diseases can spread with terrifying rapidity. An influenza **epidemic** like the one that caused so many deaths between 1918 and 1919 would spread around the world in four days rather than four months. It is next to impossible to predict what new diseases we will have to face during the 21st century.

DNA VACCINES—THE SHAPE OF THINGS TO COME?

Vaccination is an important weapon in the war against **bacteria** and **viruses**. Traditional **vaccines** consist of either weakened or heat-killed viruses, or simply **proteins** from the virus's protein coat to trigger the **immune system**. Anti-bacterial vaccines are made from bacterial **toxins** or from sugars found in the **cell** walls of the bacteria.

Dr Yen Choo of the Laboratory of Molecular Biology in Cambridge has helped to develop a technique that could be used to 'switch off' the gene that causes leukaemia.

TARGETING GENES

Vaccines have obviously been successful but they do not work against all **disease agents**. A vaccine might be effective against one **strain** of a virus but not another. Scientists are now working on vaccines that make use of the disease agent's **genes**.

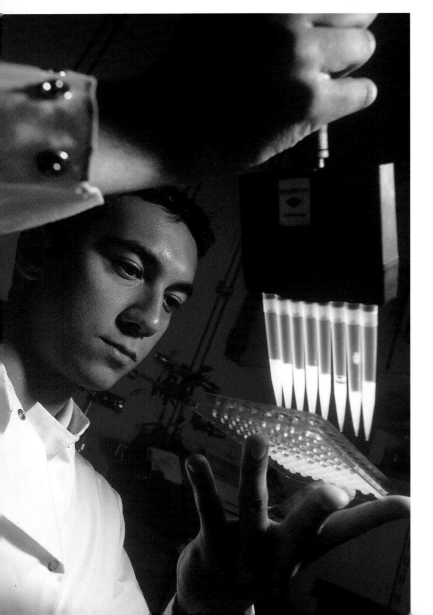

GENES AND PROTEINS

A gene is part of an organism's hereditary, or genetic, material. Each gene is like a code or set of instructions for making a protein. Proteins are large and complex molecules that perform a number of vital tasks in an organism, from controlling the rate of chemical reactions to providing structural support.

In 1990 scientists discovered that genes from other organisms could be taken up by cells in the body and used to produce proteins. A gene from a disease agent can be inserted into a circular piece of **DNA** called a **plasmid**.

When this DNA plasmid is injected into someone, the DNA serves as a blueprint for the production of the disease agent protein. Because the DNA vaccine only has the code for a small part of the disease agent it cannot become **infectious**.

IMMUNE TRIGGER

It is thought that because the disease agent's protein originates inside the host cells it triggers **antibody** production by the immune system. This immune response is in some respects superior to that produced by traditional vaccines and gives better protection against viral infections.

A CURE FOR FLU?

Much of the work on DNA vaccines has been aimed at producing an effective vaccine against influenza. Traditional anti-influenza vaccines have targeted proteins on the surface of the virus particle. But these proteins change frequently as the genes that produce them **mutate**. The DNA vaccine being developed targets a protein inside the virus that is much less likely to change.

DNA vaccines may also be used to treat people who are already suffering from viral infections, such as hepatitis or HIV. By boosting the immune response using a DNA vaccine, it is thought that the immune system could be sufficiently enhanced to kill all infected cells and wipe out the infection.

THE RISKS

The development of a DNA vaccine against HIV, the virus that causes AIDS, is one exciting possibility. The safety of DNA vaccines is being carefully monitored by researchers. One concern is whether or not the injected DNA will become incorporated into the patient's **chromosomes**, although there is no evidence so far that it does. There is also a possibility that a DNA vaccine would cause the body's immune system to attack its own cells because they are making foreign proteins. However, DNA vaccines could be the treatment of tomorrow.

BIOLOGICAL WEAPONS

Perhaps no form of warfare has been more rightly condemned than the threat to use **disease agents** deliberately as a weapon. Biological agents of warfare are living organisms, whatever their nature, intended to cause disease or death.

The effects of biological agents vary greatly, depending on the properties of the disease-causing **micro-organisms**, the method of transmitting the agent to people and how susceptible the people are to the disease. Depending on which organism is used there may be a delay of a few days to a few weeks before any effect is seen. The result of an attack would also depend on how **contagious** the agent is.

POTENTIAL WEAPONS

Viruses, **bacteria** and **fungi** can all be used as biological weapons. They could be used against humans, domestic animals or plants. To be useful for biological warfare, the micro-organisms would have to be relatively easy to grow in the laboratory. They must be able to survive in air for several hours or in water or food for several days, and they must cause severe, but not necessarily fatal, illness for a long time. The viral diseases influenza, yellow fever and dengue fever and the bacterial diseases anthrax, plague and dysentery all meet these demands for attacks on humans.

DEPLOYING THE DISEASE

Biological weapons have often been regarded as cheap and simple substitutes for nuclear or chemical weapons for use against populations in large areas. Spray devices mounted on aircraft or ships could be used to release the weapon. Large areas could be covered using equipment like this. In theory a single aircraft spraying a deadly organism could kill half the people in an area the size of New York City. Another method would be to infect a city's water supply.

NO PROTECTION

The most efficient
protection against a
biological weapon would
be **vaccination**, but since

A team of United Nations investigators attempt to get access to an Iraqi biological-weapons plant. Iraq has been accused of producing large stocks of biological weapons.

this would have to be carried out weeks or months in advance
of an attack, and as there would be no knowledge of the type
of organism to be used, it isn't a realistic option.

In 1972 an international convention was presented forbidding
the production, storage and use of biological weapons.
However, it was not considered a guarantee against the
development of biological weapons, because there were few
controls and many ways in which research and production of
biological agents could be hidden. Within only a few years
there were a number of allegations that the treaty had been
broken. Recently, the possibility of using genetic engineering
(deliberately changing the genetic material of an organism) to
produce powerful and dangerous new biological weapons has
emerged.

GLOSSARY

antibiotic   substance produced by or obtained from certain bacteria or fungi that can be used to kill or inhibit the growth of disease-causing micro-organisms

antibody   defensive protein produced by an organism in response to the presence of foreign or invading substances such as the proteins found on viruses or bacteria

bacterium   (plural bacteria) any of a large group of single-celled organisms which have no organized nucleus

biofilm   colony of billions of bacteria living on the surface of something that can provide them with water and nutrients. The biofilm colony produces a protective slimy coat.

cell   the basic unit of life. Cells can exist as independent life forms, such as bacteria and protists, or form tissues in more complicated life forms, such as muscle cells and nerve cells in animals.

chromosome   thread-like structures that become visible in the nucleus of a cell just before it divides. Chromosomes carry the genes that determine the characteristics of an organism.

compound   substance formed from two or more chemical elements

contagious   describes a disease that can be transmitted by contact between one organism and another

disease agent   organism, such as a bacterium, that can cause disease

DNA   (deoxyribonuleic acid) genetic material of almost all living things with the exception of some viruses. DNA consists of two long chains of nucleotides joined together in a double helix.

epidemic   disease that affects many people at the same time and spreads rapidly by infection

evolve   in biology, to develop a characteristic over a period of time as a result of mutation and natural selection

fungus   any of a group of spore-producing organisms that includes mushrooms and moulds

gene   the unit of heredity. A gene is a length of DNA and a number of genes are carried on a chromosome. A gene is the set of instructions for assembling a protein from amino acids

helminth   any of a group of parasitic worms that includes flukes and tapeworms

immune system cells of the body that give protection against invasion by foreign micro-organisms such as bacteria and viruses. These include cells that directly attack invading organisms and cells that destroy infected body cells.

immunization   giving immunity to a disease by introducing a weakened or killed form of a virus into the body. This triggers the immune system's response to that disease, making it ready to deal effectively with the active form of the virus if encountered.

infectious   describes something that is capable of causing infection or is caused by an infection (an infection is an invasion of an organism by disease-causing micro-organisms)

interferon protein produced by cells in the body that are infected by viruses. It travels to other non-infected cells and helps to protect them from infection.

microbe another name for a micro-organism

micro-organism any microscopic living thing, such as bacteria and protists

mutation change in the genes produced by a change in DNA as it is copied during cell division. Most mutations are harmful to the organism.

mycosis the growth of a fungus on or in the body

nutrient any nutritious substance found in food

pandemic epidemic that is spread over a wide geographical area

parasite one organism living on another and benefiting at the expense of it

plasmid circular strand of DNA found in bacteria that is separate from the main chromosome DNA

protein one of a group of complex organic molecules that perform a variety of essential tasks in living things, including providing structure and controlling the rates of chemical reactions

protist any single-celled eukaryote that is a member of the kingdom Protista

quarantine period of time during which a person or animal suspected of carrying an infectious disease is kept isolated to prevent the spread of the disease

radiation energy transmitted in the form of waves or particles as a result of the breakdown of a radioactive substance

rupture to break open or burst

spleen organ of the body, part of its job is to destroy old or damaged red blood cells

spore resting state of a bacterium, entered when conditions are unfavourable. A spore can resist hostile conditions for long periods of time.

strain a group of organisms of one species that have distinctive characteristics but are not sufficiently different to be considered a separate species

symptom any change in mind or body that indicates that someone is suffering from a disease

synthetic describes something that is produced by artificial means rather than naturally

toxin poisonous substance produced by an organism such as a bacterium

vaccination giving a vaccine in order to give protection from a disease

vaccine weakened or killed form of a bacterium or virus that causes disease, given to stimulate the immune system to produce antibodies against the disease

vector the path by which a disease causing micro-organism travels from one host to another. Biting insects are a common vector of disease.

virulent describes the disease causing ability of a micro-organism

virus infective particle, usually consisting of a molecule of nucleic acid in a protein coat

INDEX

AIDS (acquired immune deficiency syndrome) 5, 6, 12-13
anthrax 44
antibiotic resistance 24-5, 38, 39, 41
antibiotics 22, 24-5, 27, 28, 38
antibodies 8-9, 10, 11, 31, 33, 35, 43
ascaris worms 36
athlete's foot 28

babies 11, 19
bacteria/bacterial diseases 4, 5, 18, 20-7, 38, 40, 42, 44
biofilms 22-3
biological weapons 44-5
blood flukes 36

candida 28
cells 5, 8, 12, 22, 33
chicken pox 4
chloroquine 34
cholera 5, 20, 21
chromosomes 43
Clostridium perfringens 21
colostrum 11
common cold 4, 5, 6
cowpox 18
Cryptococcus 28, 29

dengue fever 7, 44
dental plaque 22, 23
disease agents 4, 5, 6, 14, 40, 42, 43, 44
DNA 38, 42-3
DNA vaccine 35, 43
dysentery 44

Ebola virus 5, 41
emerging diseases 40-1
epidemics 16-17, 41

food poisoning 4, 21, 25
fungi 4, 24, 28-9, 40, 44

gametocytes 33
gene exchange 17, 25
genes 38, 42, 43
genetic engineering 45
glands 8, 39

Hanta virus 41
helminths 4, 36-7, 40
hepatitis 5, 43
herpes 6, 7
histoplasmosis 29
HIV (human immunodeficiency virus) 12, 13, 41, 43
hydrophobia see rabies

immune system 5, 8, 10, 22, 28, 31, 33, 39, 42, 43
immunity 9, 10, 11, 15, 18
immunization 10-11, 19
infectious diseases 4, 5, 43
influenza 4, 6-7, 11, 16-17, 41, 43, 44
interferons 8

Jenner, Edward 18

kala-azar 30
kuru 7

Lassa fever 5, 7
Legionnaire's disease 41
leishmaniasis 30

malaria 5, 30, 32-5
MDR-TB (multiple drug resistant tuberculosis) 27
measles 4, 6, 9, 11
meningitis 28, 29
merozoites 32, 33, 34, 35
micro-organisms 4, 5, 22, 24, 44
microbe identification 40, 41
mutations 13, 38, 43
mycosis 28
mycotoxins 28

nutrients 20, 22

pandemics 18
parasites 4, 6, 30, 31, 32-3, 34, 35, 36-7
passive immunization 11
penicillin 24
plague 44
plasmids 38, 42-3
Plasmodium 30, 32, 33, 34
polio 6

polio vaccine 11
proteins 8, 31, 35, 42, 43
protists 4, 30, 32, 40
Pseudomonas aeruginosa 22, 23

quarantine 15, 19
quinine 34

rabies 6, 14-15
reservoir hosts 6
respiratory syncytial virus 11
river blindness 5

salmonella 21, 25
schistosomiasis 4, 36-7
sleeping sickness 5, 30, 31
slimes see biofilms
smallpox 18-19
spores 20, 21, 32
sporotrichosis 28
sporozoites 32, 33, 34-5
Staphylococcus aureus 21
strains 27, 38
streptococcus 39
symptoms 10, 14, 15, 18, 19, 20, 26, 29, 31, 40

T cells 33
tapeworms 36, 37
TB (tuberculosis) 5, 20, 26-7, 41
tetanus 20
toxins 20, 21, 42
transmission of diseases 6-7, 13, 14, 17, 18-19, 30, 31, 32
trypanosomes 30, 31

Unexplained Illness Working Group 41

vaccines/vaccination 10, 11, 15, 18, 27, 34, 42-3, 45
vectors 6-7, 32, 37
viruses/viral infections 4, 6-17, 24, 38, 40, 42, 43, 44

WHO (World Health Organization) 19, 27

yellow fever 44